KNOW-IT-ALLS

TREASURY OF Animals AND Nature

Learning Horizons

©2003 Learning Horizons
One American Road, Cleveland, OH 44144
Made in China

visit us at: www.learninghorizons.com

DINOSAURS!
written by Jay Johnson
illustrated by Greg Harris

WHALES!
written by Irene Trimble
illustrated by Greg Harris
reviewed by Lisa Mielke, Department of Education, New York Aquarium

SEALS!
written by Ellen Catala
illustrated by Greg Harris
reviewed by Dr. Edward M. Spevak, Assistant Curator of Mammals at the Bronx Zoo

SHARKS!
written by Irene Trimble
illustrated by Mike Maydak
reviewed by Marcelo R. de Carvalho, Department of Icthyology, American Museum of Natural History
art reviewed by Lisa Mielke, Department of Education, New York Aquarium

FISH!
written by Christopher Nicholas
illustrated by Jean Cassels
reviewed by Lisa Mielke, Department of Education, New York Aquarium

SNAKES!
written by Christopher Nicholas
illustrated by Mike Maydak
reviewed by Dr. John Behler, Curator of Herpetology at the Bronx Zoo

SPIDERS!
written by Christopher Nicholas
illustrated by Mike Maydak
reviewed by Dr. Art Evans, Insect Zoo Director, Natural History Museum of Los Angeles County

BUGS!
written by Christopher Nicholas
illustrated by Mike Maydak

BUTTERFLIES!
written by Darlene Freeman
illustrated by Mike Maydak
reviewed by Louis Sorkin, Department of Entomology, American Museum of Natural History

HORSES!
written by Dennis Shealy
illustrated by Stephen Schreiber
reviewed by Frank Indiviglio, Zoologist

KITTENS!
written by Christopher Nicholas
illustrated by Illustrated Alaskan Moose Studios
reviewed by Frank Indiviglio, Zoologist

WILD CATS!
written by Diane Muldrow
illustrated by Greg Harris

TABLE OF CONTENTS

DINOSAURS!

MILLIONS OF YEARS AGO

You see a lot of dinosaurs in movies and on TV shows. But do you think those are real dinosaurs?

DINO TIMELINE

First Dinosaurs Appear
225 MYA   **208 MYA**

MYA = Millon Years Ago | **Triassic Period** | **Jurassic Period**

Real dinosaurs are *extinct*—that means they are dead and gone forever. Dinosaurs were animals, in the same big group as birds and crocodiles. They lived on earth a very long time ago—way before people.

144 MYA		Dinosaurs Become Extinct 65 MYA	First People Appear 40,000 YEARS AGO
Cretaceous Period			Today

3

ROCKY RECORDS

How do we know dinosaurs really lived on earth? Scientists called **paleontologists** study **fossils**. Fossils are the remains of things that lived millions of years ago. These remains have become part of rocks buried in the earth.

There are many fossils of dinosaur tracks, bones, skin, and even eggs! In fact, scientists find a new dino fossil about every six weeks!

Over 700 kinds of dinosaurs have been identified. Most of them have been found in the past 25 years.

DINOSAUR MEALS

POLACANTHUS (PLANT-EATER)

Most kinds of dinosaurs ate only *plants*. Many of them had gigantic bodies with huge stomachs. And some had long necks to reach leafy treetops.

Other kinds of dinos ate only *meat*—lizards, insects, and other dinosaurs. Most meat-eaters ran on two feet, rather than four. They were fast runners, which helped them catch their dinner. Some meat-eaters were big, but some were as small as chickens!

BARYONYX (MEAT-EATER)

A few kinds of dinosaurs ate both meat and plants. They liked variety!

7

ALLOSAURUS
(AL-o-SAW-rus)

Allosaurus was fierce. It was one of the biggest, strongest meat-eaters of its time. It had large teeth with edges like saw blades. Its head was as big as a first-grader!

This dinosaur weighed up to 2 tons (1.8 metric tons). It was about 35 feet (11 m) long and 9 feet (3 m) tall at the hips.

Some people believe that *Allosaurus* looked for food—usually other dinosaurs—in a group of hunters called a **pack.**

WHEN IT LIVED:

About 150 million years ago, Jurassic Period

FOSSILS FOUND IN:

Colorado, Wyoming, Utah, Oklahoma, New Mexico

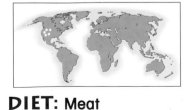

DIET: Meat

9

BRACHIOSAURUS
(BRACK-ee-o-SAW-rus)

Like the giraffe, this dinosaur had long front legs and a superlong neck so it could nibble leaves from the highest tree branches. Its head rose up to 60 feet (18 m) off the ground—that's as high as a four-story building!

This four-legged dinosaur was a giant, weighing up to 80 tons (72.5 metric tons). *Brachiosaurus* grew an amazing 100 feet (30.5 m) long. The length of three of these dinosaurs would equal one football field!

Brachiosaurus may have had a good sense of smell because it had huge nostrils—on top of its head!

STEGOSAURUS
(STEG-o-SAW-rus)

Stegosaurus had a tail as long as its elephant-sized body (about 30 feet or 9 meters). With four sharp spines, the tail could be used as a great club to fight off meat-eaters!

Stegosaurus also had a double row of triangular plates from its neck to its tail. The plates probably helped protect the dinosaur from being eaten! Some of the plates were as small as saucers. Others were as big as truck wheels!

WHEN IT LIVED:
About 150 million years ago, Jurassic Period

FOSSILS FOUND IN:
Western North America

DIET: Plants

ALLOSAURUS

13

IGUANODON
(ig-WAN-o-don)

Chomp, chomp, chomp! *Iguanodon* was the first plant-eating dino whose fossils were discovered in modern times. They were found in England in 1825.

Iguanodons traveled together in herds that grazed along the edges of swamps and lakes. Their strong grinding teeth chewed up juicy ferns and reeds.

This dinosaur was heavy. It weighed up to 6 tons (5.5 metric tons). It was 33 feet (10 m) long and taller than two grownups balancing on each other's shoulders!

15

VELOCIRAPTOR

(ve-LOSS-uh-RAP-ter)

Velociraptor lived in deserts. It had large eyes. It may have needed big eyes to hunt at night. It probably ate lizards and other small animals, tiny baby dinosaurs (called **hatchlings**), and eggs.

PROTOCERATOPS

16

Velociraptor means "swift robber." This dino was smart and fast! It had a large slashing toe and hand claws. Its second-toe claw was 4 inches (10 cm) long. *Velociraptor's* body grew to about 6 feet (2 m) long, the size of a large dog. Very bad doggie!

WHEN IT LIVED:
About 75–80 million years ago, Cretaceous Period

FOSSILS FOUND IN:
Mongolia and China

DIET: You know...meat!

TRICERATOPS
(try-SAIR-a-tops)

Knights in the Middle Ages used armor to protect themselves in battle. *Triceratops* also had an armor-covered face for protection—and three sharp horns! Its name means "three-horned head."

Triceratops also had a big frill of bone. This frill may have protected the neck and shoulders from attacks. Or it may have just been for show, like a peacock's feathers.

18

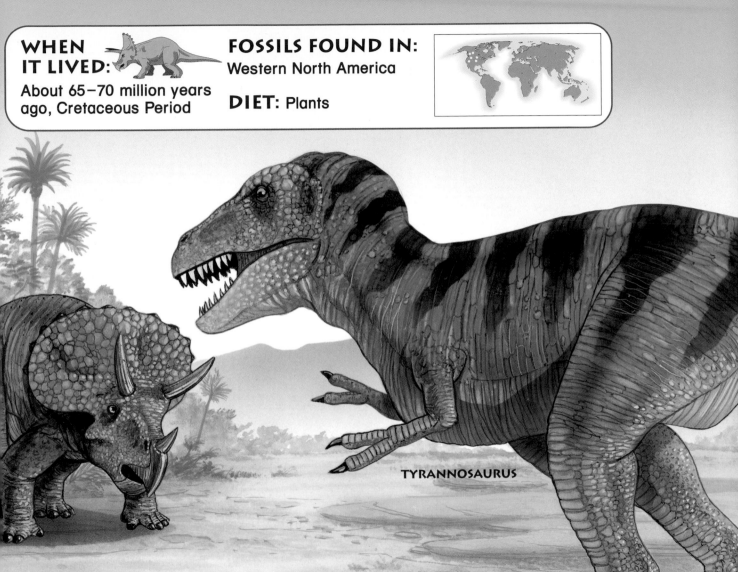

TYRANNOSAURUS

This dino chewed on ferns, palms, and other plants. And it ate a lot of them! *Triceratops* weighed almost 6 tons (5.5 metric tons) and was about 30 feet (9 m) long. That's as big as an elephant!

19

WHEN IT LIVED:
About 67–100 million years ago, Cretaceous Period

FOSSILS FOUND IN:
North America and Asia

DIET: Meat

TYRANNOSAURUS
(tie-RAN-o-SAW-rus)

Tyrannosaurus was the fiercest meat-eating dinosaur. It wasn't the biggest, but it was huge—7 tons (6.5 metric tons) of charging monster. At over 40 feet (12 m) long, it was a smart killer with sharp eyesight.

This dinosaur's head was over 5 feet (1.5 m) long. Its muscular mouth was filled with 50 sharp, jagged teeth. The biggest teeth were the size of bananas! Its front limbs were strong, but they were so short they couldn't even reach up to its mouth.

21

SINOSAUROPTERYX

(SIN-o-sar-OP-terix)

Sinosauropteryx was a birdlike dinosaur with big eyes like an owl and a narrow head like a pheasant. It was a little over 3 feet (1 m) long and about as tall as a grownup's knee. *Sinosauropteryx* was a swift little creature that probably ate insects and lizards as well as plants that grew close to the ground.

WHEN IT LIVED: About 135 million years ago, Cretaceous Period

FOSSILS FOUND IN: China

DIET: Meat and plants

Did you know that today's birds are called "living dinosaurs"? That's because they developed from small dinosaurs, like *Sinosauropteryx*, millions of years ago!

Why did all the dinos disappear? Did the great meteor that hit the earth kill them? Or did they vanish because of disease?

No one knows for certain!

KNOW-IT-ALLS

WHALES!

SPLASH!

Imagine seeing an animal the size of a fire truck jumping out of the water and landing with a tremendous *SPLASH!* If you're lucky enough to go whale watching, that's just one of the amazing things you might see a whale do!

gray whale

There are 79 different species of whale in the world. The largest of them can weigh more than 30 elephants! Yet some of these awesome creatures will allow humans to touch them.

MAGNIFICENT MAMMALS

Whales are mammals, not fish. Like all warm-blooded creatures, whales have to breathe air to survive. They swim to the water's surface and breathe through a **blowhole**. A blowhole is like a nose on top of its head!

blue whale

Whales also have hair on their bodies and give birth to live young. Baby whales, called **calves**, drink rich milk from their mother's body. Some calves may gain as much as 200 pounds (91 kg) a day!

HOW THEY EAT

There are two kinds of whales: baleen whales and toothed whales. Baleen whales have a set of brushes in their mouths called **baleen plates**. They use the baleen to strain tiny plants and animals, called **plankton**, out of the water. Toothed whales have teeth to catch their food.

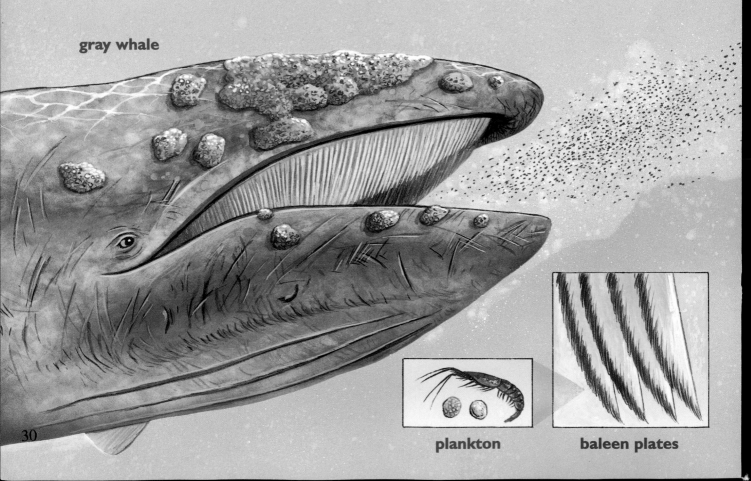

gray whale

plankton

baleen plates

Another way to tell whales apart is by looking at the tops of their heads! Baleen whales have two blow holes. Toothed whales have only one blow hole.

killer whale

GRAY WHALES

Gray Whales travel from the cold Bering Sea in Alaska to California, Baja, and Mexico to have their babies. This 13,000 mile (21,000 km) journey is the longest **migration** of any mammal. When a baby Gray Whale is born in these warm waters, it is 16 feet (5 m) long! That's a big baby!

 **Facts**

- Size: 46 feet (14 m) long, 35 tons (31.5 metric tons)
- Type: baleen
- Diet: crabs & other mud-dwelling creatures
- Found in the Northern Hemisphere

Gray Whales are the only baleen whales that feed from the bottom of the ocean. They suck in huge amounts of crabs, worms, and other animals that live in the mud.

BLUE WHALES

These enormous whales are the largest animals on Earth! Blue Whales can grow longer than two school buses put together. They can eat up to four tons (3.5 metric tons) of plankton and small shrimp, called **krill**, a day—that's like eating 32,000 hamburgers!

 **Facts**

- Size: 85 feet (26 m) long, 100 tons (90 metric tons)
- Type: baleen
- Diet: plankton, krill
- Found in the Northern Hemisphere

Like most baleen whales, Blue Whales feed in cold waters and then travel to warmer parts of the world to breed and have their calves.

KILLER WHALES

Killer Whales are swift, deadly predators that live and hunt in family groups called **pods**. They swim at speeds of up to 34 miles per hour (55 kmh) and have 48 curved teeth for biting into their prey. They have even been known to come right out of the water to grab a seal on a beach!

Killer Whales are also called **orcas**. There is no record of an orca ever attacking a person in the wild— but they do eat other mammals!

 **Facts**

- Size: 32 feet (9.7 m) long, 8 tons (7.2 metric tons)
- Type: toothed
- Diet: fish, seals, sea turtles, dolphins, sharks, other whales
- Found worldwide

BELUGA WHALES

Beluga Whales live in cold waters where there is lots of ice, so their snowy white coloring makes them very hard to see. Believe it or not, they are sometimes attacked by polar bears!

 Facts

- Size: 16 feet (5 m) long, 1 ton (0.9 metric tons)
- Type: toothed
- Diet: fish
- Found in the Arctic

NARWHALS

Male Narwhals have a long spiral tusk that looks like a sword. This tusk is really a tooth that can grow up to 9 feet (3 m) long!

female narwhal

 **Facts**

- Size: 16 feet (5 m) long, 2 tons (1.8 metric tons)
- Type: toothed
- Diet: squid, fish, crab, shrimp
- Found in the Arctic

SPERM WHALES

You can tell Sperm Whales by their huge square heads, dark color, and wrinkled skin. They also have the largest brain in the world. An adult Sperm Whale's brain can weigh up to 20 pounds (9 kg)!

Sperm Whales sometimes battle and eat giant squid!
You can often see round marks left on their heads and
bodies by the struggling squid's tentacles.

 **Facts**

- Size: 59 feet (17.8 m) long,
  60 tons (54 metric tons)
- Type: toothed
- Diet: squid, fish
- Found worldwide

HUMPBACK WHALES

Can you tell a whale by its tail? You can if it's a Humpback! The two halves of a whale's tail are called **flukes**. No two Humpbacks have the same fluke markings, just as no two people have the same fingerprints. Humpback Whales have flukes that are 18 feet (6 m) wide!

 **Facts**

- Size: 49 feet (15 m) long, 45 tons (40.5 metric tons)
- Type: baleen
- Diet: krill
- Found worldwide

Many whales make clicks, squeaks, and other vocalizations using their blow holes. Humpback Whales are called "singing whales" because their mating songs are so long and beautiful!

43

BOWHEAD WHALES

Bowhead Whales are the only large whales that spend their entire lives in the Arctic. Bowhead Whales can live in very cold waters because they have the thickest layer of fat of any whale! The fat, called **blubber**, keeps whales warm and cozy.

 **Facts**

- Size: 59 feet (17.8 m),
  110 tons (99 metric tons)
- Type: baleen
- Diet: small fish, krill, plankton
- Found from the Arctic Ocean
  to the Bering Sea

Bowhead whales also have the longest baleen structure of any whale. With baleen plates that are 9 feet (3 m) long, they can scoop up a lot of krill and plankton!

BET YOU DIDN'T KNOW...

A newborn Blue Whale calf is 24 feet (7.2 m) long and weighs 2 tons (1.8 metric tons). It's the biggest baby in the world!

Sperm Whales spit up a substance called **ambergris**. It was once used to make perfume!

The Bowhead Whale has the biggest tongue—it can weigh over 1 ton (0.9 metric ton).

In the past, whalers called Gray Whales "devil fish" because the females used to destroy small boats that got between them and their calves.

Whales make sounds that help them locate food and find their way through the ocean. This is called **echolocation**.

Humans are still trying to unlock the many secrets of whales. We are just beginning to learn how deeply whales can dive, how far they can travel, and how intelligent these amazing creatures really are!

KNOW-IT-ALLS

SEALS!

They live both in the sea and on land. Some of them weigh as much as rhinoceroses.

WHAT ARE THEY?

(HINT: TURN THE PAGE TO FIND OUT...)

Answer:

SEALS! ARE SEALS FISH?

No. They are a kind of ocean mammal that scientists call a **pinniped**—which means "fin foot." Like all mammals, including people, seal babies drink milk from their mothers. There are three main kinds of seal.

1. Fur seals and sea lions have ears you can see. They are called **eared seals**.

California Sea Lion

Stellar Sea Lion

Northern Fur Seal

New Zealand Fur Seal

2. **Earless seals**, such as harbor seals, bearded seals, and ringed seals, have ears that don't show on the outside.

Harbor Seal

Bearded Seal

Ringed Seal

Kinds of

- eared seals
- earless seals
- walruses

3. **Walruses** have tusks!

Seals range in size from the 4 ton (3,600 kg) southern elephant seal to the 150 pound (68 kg) Baikal seal.

53

DO SEALS WALK OR SWIM?

Both! But they swim much more gracefully than they walk. Their soft, smooth bodies glide through water. Eared seals swim by moving their powerful front flippers. Earless seals and walruses swim by flapping their wide back flippers.

Water Speeds

- Slowest–walruses travel up to 6 miles per hour (10 kmph)
- Fastest–fur seals and seal lions travel up to 34 mph (55 kmph)

California Sea Lion

Harbor Seal

On land, they move much more slowly. Fur seals, sea lions, and walruses can pull their back flippers under their bodies to use as legs—so they can walk. Earless seals, however, can't use their rear flippers for walking—so they use their front flippers to drag their bodies.

55

HOW DO SEALS STAY WARM?

They have a thick layer of fat under their skin called **blubber**. The fat keeps their insides warm. And they don't seem to mind cold on their thick skin. Many seals cover themselves with snow and sleep on ice!

A walrus's skin is 2 inches (5 cm) thick!

Hooded Seal (male)

Fur seals have a layer of blubber *and* two fur coats to keep them warm. The bottom coat is soft and thick so it traps body heat. While the top coat is coarse and oily so it keeps out water.

Bearded Seal

All seals **molt**—which means they shed their old coats each year to reveal new ones underneath.

57

CAN SEALS SEE UNDERWATER?

Yes! In fact, seals can see very well in the depths of the ocean where human eyes would see only blackness. Their tear glands put a film of fine clear oil over their eyes. The oil protects against saltwater and blowing snow.

On land, everything they look at is a little blurry. They sometimes mistake a motionless polar bear for a mound of snow. Knowing this, polar bears stand very still if a seal they are stalking looks their way!

WHAT DO SEALS EAT?

Most eat seafood—fish, shellfish, and small ocean animals such as squid. Some seals eat other kinds of animals. The leopard seal eats penguins and seal pups, as well as fish!

Sea lions often swallow rocks. Over 100 were found in the stomach of one animal!

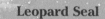

Leopard Seal

Walruses eat huge amounts of food—about 100 pounds (45 kg) a day. They root in the mud at the bottom of the ocean for shellfish. But rogue walruses, which are very rare, eat meat—especially seals!

When fishing is poor, seals can always live off their blubber for a while—but not forever. They need that blubber to stay warm!

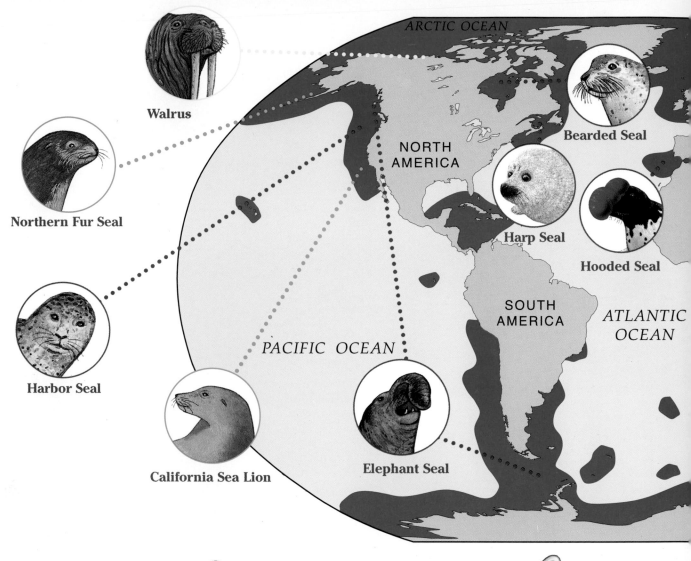

Walrus

Northern Fur Seal

Harbor Seal

California Sea Lion

ARCTIC OCEAN

NORTH AMERICA

Bearded Seal

Harp Seal

Hooded Seal

SOUTH AMERICA

ATLANTIC OCEAN

PACIFIC OCEAN

Elephant Seal

WHERE DO SEALS LIVE?

All over the world, but they prefer places that are cold.
Most seals live in salt water. However, the Baikal seal lives
in Lake Baikal in Russia. And a few other kinds of seal also
live in freshwater lakes in very cold regions.

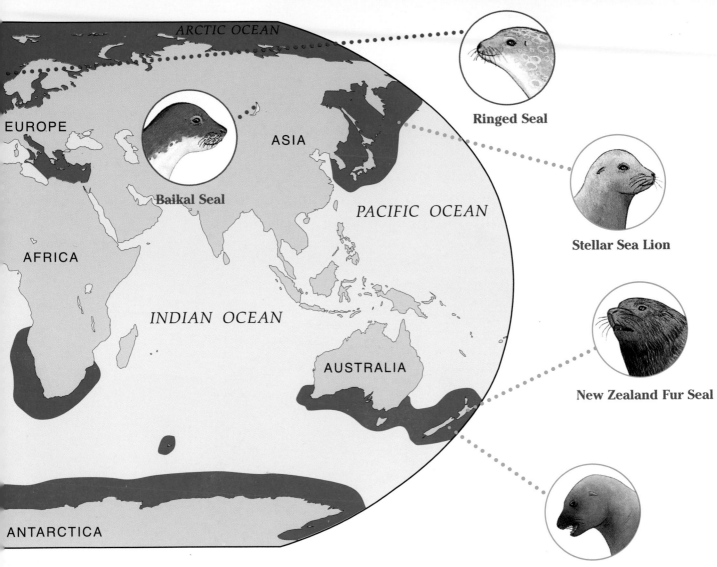

Ringed Seal

Stellar Sea Lion

New Zealand Fur Seal

New Zealand Sea Lion

Baikal Seal

ARCTIC OCEAN

EUROPE

ASIA

PACIFIC OCEAN

AFRICA

INDIAN OCEAN

AUSTRALIA

ANTARCTICA

In general, eared seals meet in big groups, called **rookeries**.
Earless seals are more likely to live alone or in small groups.
But there are exceptions to this rule.

All walruses, except for rogue walruses, live in large groups.

WHAT ABOUT BABIES?

Mother seals give birth to one baby, called a **pup**, about once a year. The mother usually goes to the place where she was born to have her pup.

All seal pups are born either on land or on ice. Harp seals, for example, will only bear their pups on ice.

Great hooded seal pups drink up to 20 pounds (9 kg) of milk every day for four days after they are born!

Hooded Seal

Earless seals that have babies on ice floes do not hunt for food while they are nursing their young. They just live off their fat! These seals do not let their pups out of sight until they are weaned, which is usually 4 days to 8 weeks after birth.

Mother seals recognize their babies by their cry and their smell. The stellar sea lion drops her newborn pup over and over on rocks until it cries, so she can learn to recognize its voice!

New Zealand Sea Lion

Eared seals may nurse their pups from a few months to a year. The mother often leaves her pups from time to time to feed at sea.

Eared seal pups are often in danger of being trampled by adult males, called **bulls**. Some bulls, which may be five times larger than the females, will actually attack and kill pups that get in their way!

Walruses are very good mothers. They keep a close eye on their babies, called **calves**, for two years!

67

DO SEALS HAVE ANY ENEMIES?

Yes—polar bears, sharks, killer whales, and people. That is why some seals have pups on ice floes—which are hard for their enemies to reach! Walruses are so huge that they have no enemies except for people.

Human hunters in the 18th and 19th Centuries killed so many seals that many species almost became extinct! If only those hunters had followed the wisdom of the Inuit, the native people of the Arctic. The Inuit valued seals because they depended upon them for food, clothes, and some housing materials. They never killed more animals than they needed to survive!

Today, many countries have laws that protect seals.

BET YOU DIDN'T KNOW. . .

A walrus's body turns from white to red when it gets out of the water and lies in the sun!

Male elephant seals may go without food for 100 days during breeding season.

The greatest danger to seals now is caused by people taking too many fish from the ocean . . . which doesn't leave enough food for seals!

A harbor seal at the New England Aquarium learned to say his name, "Hoover," and phrases such as "Come over here" and "Get out of here!"

Seals in danger of being eaten by polar bears don't sleep soundly. They wake up every few minutes to look around.

Seals have the same bones in their flippers that humans have in their hands.

WHEN A MOTHER SEAL HAS BEEN AWAY, SHE GREETS HER PUP BY BRUSHING NOSES. YOU MIGHT SAY, THEIR LOVE IS...

71

SEALED WITH A KISS!

72 **Harp Seal**

KNOW-IT-ALLS

SHARKS!

Long before dinosaurs ruled the land...

SHARKS

hunted the seas. They have survived on earth for 400 million years!

Megalodon

Great White

The now extinct Megalodon shark lived 15 million years ago. It was 40 feet (12 m) long, and its jaws were so large, a man could stand inside them!

Today there are over 375 different kinds, or **species**, of sharks. Marine biologists, the scientists who study ocean life, are still discovering more!

POWERFUL HUNTERS

Sharks have skeletons made of soft, flexible **cartilage** instead of hard bone. (The end of your nose is made of cartilage.)

Instead of smooth scales, sharks have very tough skin covered with tiny barbs called **dermal denticles**. And they use their strong jaws and many rows of very sharp teeth for biting and tearing!

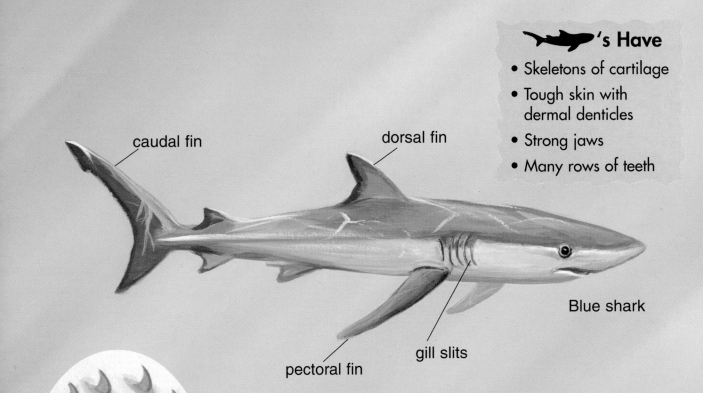

caudal fin

dorsal fin

's Have

- Skeletons of cartilage
- Tough skin with dermal denticles
- Strong jaws
- Many rows of teeth

Blue shark

gill slits

pectoral fin

dermal denticles

fish scales

These characteristics plus a huge appetite make the shark one of the most fierce fish! It's no wonder that these predators cruise the seas and oceans without fear…they have almost no natural enemies—except other sharks and humans!

77

SHARK SENSES

Sharks use sight, smell, hearing, touch, and taste. Their sense of smell is excellent. They can smell blood in the water from over a mile (1.6 km) away!

White-tip reef shark

Tiger shark

Sharks also have sensors, called **ampullae** (am-PULL-ee), in their snouts, and sensitive hairs and channels, called a **lateral line system**, along their sides. These extra senses help them find distant or unseen prey and navigate through the ocean.

79

SHARK ATTACK

A shark begins to look for its prey when it is within about 100 feet (31 m). At this point, the shark circles the victim slowly and may even bump into it a few times to see how strong it is. Then the shark quickly picks up speed as it closes in for the attack!

Silky shark

The attack begins as the shark clamps down on its victim with powerful jaws, and shakes its head from side to side to tear out a bite! The smell of blood can cause other sharks to join the attack. They wildly take bites of the wounded fish or animal. This is called a **feeding frenzy**.

BLUE SHARKS

Many shark species travel great distances, like migrating birds. Blue sharks may be the farthest ranging, swimming up to 4,000 miles (6,400 km) in about a year!

Like most sharks, baby Blue sharks are born ready to swim. Young sharks are called **pups**. Female Blue sharks can give birth to more than 50 pups at a time!

Blue 's

- Length: 12 feet (4 m)
- Diet: fish, squid, and dead whales
- Blue sharks live in warm tropical waters and follow warm ocean currents all over the world.

A few species of shark lay eggs, like other fish.

HAMMERHEAD SHARKS

These sharks swim in gigantic packs of 150 or more! They have wide, flat heads that help them slice through the water.

The hammer-shaped heads of these sharks can be up to 3 feet (1 m) wide, with eyes set on each end. (Imagine having eyes that far apart!) As they swim, hammerheads swing their heads from side to side. This motion may help them see more of their surroundings.

85

TIGER SHARKS

Tiger sharks feed on almost every other fish and mammal in the sea. In fact, they will take a bite out of ANYTHING! License plates, rolls of tar paper, tin cans, and other not-so-very-digestible items have been found in their stomachs!

Tiger sharks have curved teeth with sharp notches, like a steak knife.

Tiger Shark's

- Length: up to 18 feet (5.5 m)
- Diet: fish, sea turtles, seals, and just about anything else
- Tiger sharks can most often be seen in the Pacific and Indian Oceans.

Tiger sharks have stripes like a tiger. However, their stripes get lighter as they get older!

THRESHER SHARKS

Thresher sharks have the longest tails of any shark. Their tails make up half the length of their bodies!

These sharks move very quickly. They use their long tails to slap schools of small fish. Then they eat the stunned fish that cannot swim away!

Thresher 's

- Length: up to 20 feet (6 m)
- Diet: fish
- Thresher sharks live in warm coastal waters all over the world.

Thresher sharks are not dangerous to people—unless they get slapped by a tail!

WHALE SHARKS

These white-spotted giants are the largest sharks in the world! They grow longer than school buses!

Whale sharks feed at the surface of the water and swim so slowly that boats sometimes bump into them. They are so gentle that divers can catch rides on their backs!

Whale ⬛🦈's

- Length: up to 50 feet (15 m)
- Diet: plankton
- Whale sharks live in warm coastal waters all over the world.

They live on tiny plants and animals, called **plankton**, that drift through the sea. Whale sharks have over 4,000 teeth, but each tooth is less than 1/8 inch (3/10 cm) long.

BULL SHARKS

These dangerous sharks are very aggressive. They live in every ocean and have been known to swim hundreds of miles into freshwater rivers and lakes!

Bull sharks have been found in the Amazon River in South America, the Ganges River in India, and the Mississippi River in the United States!

Bull 's

- Length: up to 10 feet (3 m)
- Diet: fish—and just about anything else
- Bull sharks are found in warm coastal waters worldwide, and in some freshwater rivers.

GREAT WHITE SHARKS

The Great White is one of the largest predators in the sea. Its thick torpedo-shaped body can weigh 2 to 5 tons (2 to 4.5 metric tons)!

These sharks hunt alone, cruising at about 2 miles (3 km) per hour. But Great Whites are very hard for ocean scientists to track. Very little is actually known about these mysterious beasts.

Great White **'s**

- Length: up to 35 feet (11 m)
- Diet: seals, sea lions, and large fish
- Great White sharks are found all over the world—especially in Australia's Great Barrier Reef.

The Great White's triangular teeth are 2 inches (5 cm) long. Their powerful jaws are filled with many rows of these teeth!

SO MANY SHARKS

Over millions of years, sharks have learned to live in many different underwater environments. Today these silent and mysterious predators come in a variety of shapes and sizes, and they thrive in almost every sea and ocean on earth.

KNOW-IT-ALLS

Fish!

They have been living on this planet for almost a half billion years. There are more than 30,000 different kinds of them. And their home covers almost three-quarters of the earth's surface.

Tube Sponge

Red Finger Sponge

98

What are they?

(hint: turn the page to find out . . .)

What Is a Fish?

It's an animal that lives in water. Fish come in many different shapes and sizes. They can be as big as a school bus or as small as a grain of rice. They can be round like a balloon or long and thin like a pencil.

All fish have fins. A fish moves its caudal fin, or tail, from side to side to propel itself through the water. It uses its other fins to steer and to stop.

Porcupine fish

Queen Angelfish

Blue Tang

Eagle Ray

All fish also have a backbone, which makes them **vertebrates**, like us! But unlike people, fish are cold-blooded—their body temperature changes with the temperature of the water around them.

Fish bodies are usually covered with shiny little plates, called **scales**.

Barracuda

Triggerfish

Seahorse

Green Moray Eel

Most fish have two round eyes, one on each side of the head. And they can see almost all the way around themselves—without turning their heads. That comes in handy when looking for food—or trying to avoid becoming food!

Many fish have large mouths and sharp teeth—perfect for grabbing and tearing food!

Fish don't have eyelids—so they can't close their eyes!

Harlequin Tuskfish

two eyes on side of head

two nostrils

big mouth and sharp teeth

gills

scales

Even though they don't have ears like us, fish can still hear—special organs inside their bodies feel vibrations in the water.

Most fish have two nostrils, but how do they breathe underwater? With **gills**! Fish don't have lungs so they can't breathe air. But when water goes into the fish's mouth, its gills are able to remove oxygen right from the water.

Body Parts

- Fins and a tail
- Backbone
- Scales
- Two eyes on side of head
- Big mouth and sharp teeth
- No external ears
- Two nostrils
- Gills

fins and a tail

How many different kinds of fish are there?

Thousands! But they all fall into one of three basic categories.

1. **Bony fish** have skeletons made of bone, and scales cover their bodies. Most of the fish in the world are bony fish.

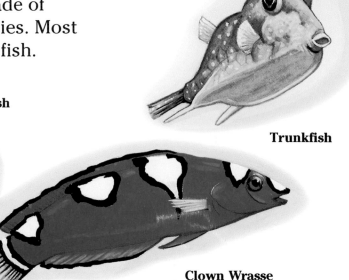

Clown Anenomefish

Trunkfish

Clown Wrasse

Blue Surgeonfish

Kinds of

- Bony fish
- Jawless fish (lampreys and hagfish)
- Sharks and rays

2. **Jawless fish** have smooth, slimy skin instead of scales. Because they don't have real jaw bones they can't bite! But lampreys do use their big, round mouths with little teeth to suck onto their prey and drink blood. Hagfish drill holes into their prey, then go inside it to eat.

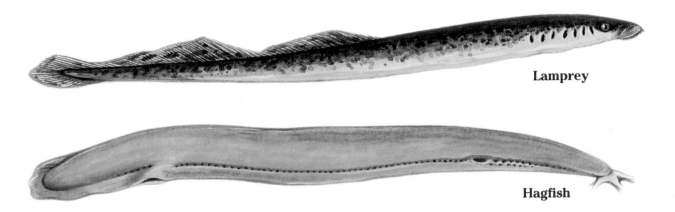

Lamprey

Hagfish

3. **Sharks and rays** have skeletons, but they are made of a tough, flexible material called cartilage instead of bone. (You have cartilage in your nose!)

Tiger Shark

Southern Stingray

Where do fish live?

They live all over the world—almost anywhere there's water! Fish can be found from the freezing waters of the arctic to the warm waters of the tropics.

Some fish live in freshwater lakes, rivers, and ponds. Others live in saltwater oceans and seas. A few fish can actually live in both salt and freshwater.

Leopard Musky

Yellow Perch

Bluegills

Half-moon Angelfish

Live In
- Lakes
- Rivers
- Ponds
- Oceans
- Seas

Blue-green chromis

Clownfish

Twospot Black Damselfish

The salmon is born in a freshwater river; then it swims to the sea and lives in saltwater!

Red Sea cleaner

107

Believe it or not, there are many strange-looking fish that can actually make their own light! Some of them live thousands of feet (or meters) below the surface!

Scientists are not sure what new and fascinating sea creatures are yet to be discovered down in the ocean's darkness!

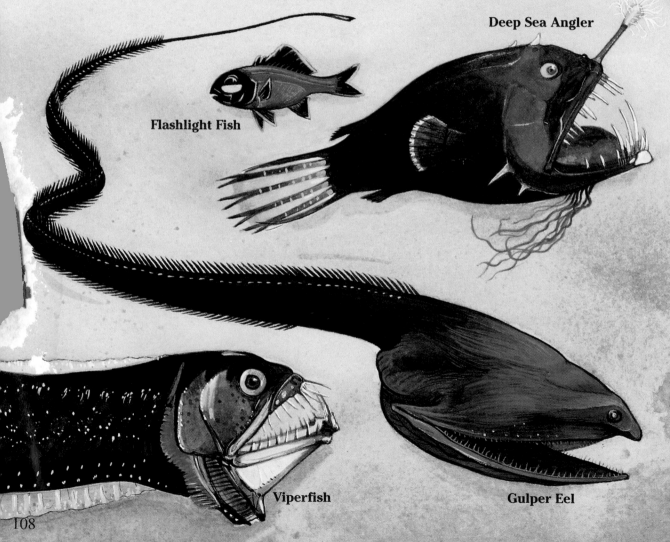

Flashlight Fish

Deep Sea Angler

Viperfish

Gulper Eel

What do fish eat?

Many fish are **carnivores**, which means they eat other animals. Some fish are **herbivores**, which means they eat only plants. And some fish eat both!

Fish that live in freshwater eat other fish, insects, and plants. Some eat very simple plants, called **algae**, that grow on rocks.

Dusky Shiner

Rosyside Dace

gills   gill rakers

Christmas Darter

Fish that eat plankton (very small water plants and animals) usually have special mouth parts called gill rakers. Fish use gill rakers to strain plankton out of the water—just like mom strains spaghetti from a pot!

Fish that live in saltwater eat other fish, sea mammals, crabs, lobsters, shrimp, plants, and algae. Some saltwater fish eat **plankton**—teeny-tiny plants and animals that float in the water.

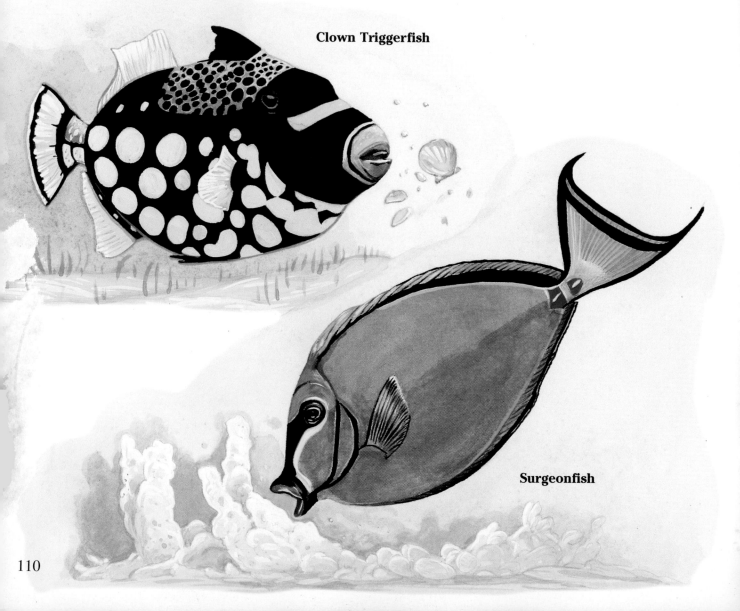

Clown Triggerfish

Surgeonfish

Some fish, like the barracuda, will eat any animal it can sink its teeth into. Yikes!

The free-loading remora likes to hitch a ride on a shark and gobble up all its leftovers!

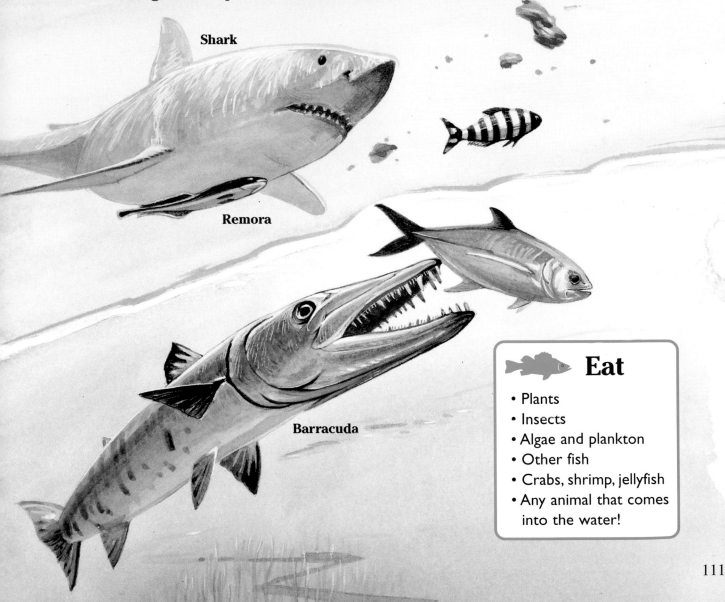

Shark

Remora

Barracuda

Eat

- Plants
- Insects
- Algae and plankton
- Other fish
- Crabs, shrimp, jellyfish
- Any animal that comes into the water!

How do meat-eaters catch their food?

Some fish swim up behind their prey, open their mouths, and swallow it whole.

Others hide out and wait for prey to swim or crawl by—and then they attack!

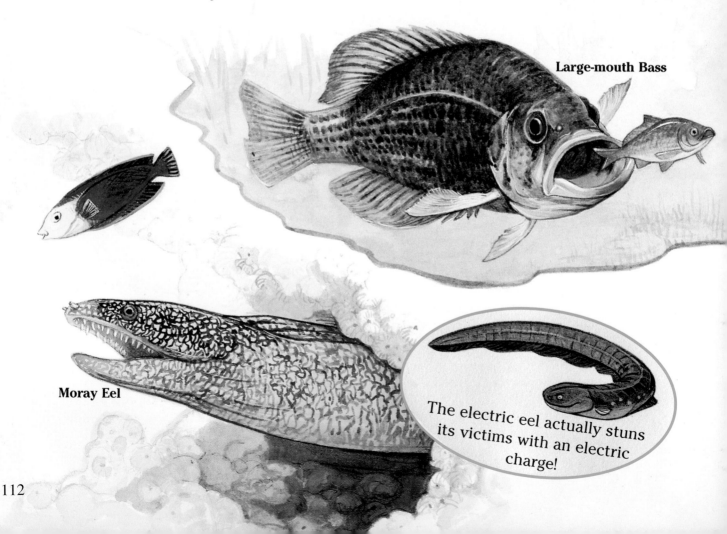

Large-mouth Bass

Moray Eel

The electric eel actually stuns its victims with an electric charge!

Some fish have special body parts that help them catch prey. Some frogfish have a built-in fishing lure to attract other fish. Swordfish and sawfish use their long noses to slash away at schools of fish.

Sawfish

Yellow Angler

How  Catch Food

- Hide and attack
- Use built-in lures
- Slash at fish with long noses
- Stun prey with electric charge

113

How do fish protect themselves?

Some fish hide. Others use **camouflage**, which means they blend right into the background.

Some fish have special coloring which scares hungry predators away. (Doesn't that spot look just like the eye of a much larger fish?)

Clown Butterflyfish

Flounder

The butterflyfish likes to hide inside a poisonous sea anemone. It is immune to the anemone's poison!

114

A few tough fish like to fight back with sharp spines or poisonous stingers. Some swallow a lot of water so they look bigger!

The flying fish can jump out of the water and glide to safety!

Flyingfish

Pufferfish

 **Defenses**

- Camouflage (Carpet Shark or Flounder)
- Spines (Porcupine Fish)
- Poison (Stingray, Scorpionfish, Stonefish)
- Hiding (Garden Eel, Butterflyfish)
- Puffing up (Puffer Fish)
- Gliding away (Flying Fish)

How do fish grow up?

Almost all female fish lay eggs. Some lay hundreds of eggs—others lay millions! Once they have laid them, many kinds of mother fish just swim away and never come back. But some hide their eggs, under sand or in mud, so that other fish won't eat them.

Mouthbrooders

A few fish take care of their eggs until they hatch. They keep them safe in their mouths or in special egg pouches within their bodies.

Many kinds of baby fish don't have scales when they hatch. But most fish grow scales within the first year.

The male seahorse actually holds the eggs in his pouch until they hatch!

Bet you didn't know...

The biggest fish in the sea is the whale shark. It can grow to be 60 feet (18 m) long and 25 tons (22 1/2 metric tons).

The largest freshwater fish is the white sturgeon of North America. It can grow up to 20 feet (6 m) long!

The blind cave fish has no eyes!

The desert pupfish can live in water as hot as a volcanic spring—96° Fahrenheit (35° C)!

Some African catfish can "walk" on dry land using their fins!

As you can see, fish are amazing!
Maybe there's a special one in your future!

120

KNOW-IT-ALLS

Snakes!

Some are as short as a pencil. Others are as long as a telephone pole! There are almost 3,000 different kinds of them in the world. And even though most are harmless, many people are afraid of them.

What are they?

(Hint: turn the
page to find out...)

WHAT IS A SNAKE?

It is a reptile! So are lizards, turtles, alligators, and crocodiles. Snakes are cold-blooded. Their body temperature depends on the temperature of the environment around them. (People are warm-blooded. Our body temperature stays at about 98.6°F (37°C) no matter where we are!)

Snakes often bask in the sun to warm themselves up, then hide in the shade to cool off.

124

A snake's body is covered with hard little plates called **scales**. It may look wet and slimy, but it is actually dry.

Scarlet Kingsnake

Snakes don't have legs—so they can't walk! They have to glide on their bellies, or move their bodies from side to side, to get where they want to go.

125

Snakes have two eyes. But they don't have eyelids—so they can't blink! Many snakes can see very well.

Rattlesnake

They don't have ears, but snakes "hear" by feeling vibrations as they slither across the ground. And they can smell with the help of their forked tongue!

One thing a snake *does* have is sharp teeth!

's **Bodies**
- Scaly skin
- No legs
- No eyelids
- No ears
- Forked tongue
- Sharp teeth

Sidewinder

Rattlesnakes have heat detectors on their faces which help them sense the body heat of another animal. Cool!

127

WHERE DO SNAKES LIVE?

Eastern Ribbon Snake

All over the world! But they especially like to be where it is warm. Snakes can be found in jungles, deserts, swamps, and forests. Sometimes they are even in your own backyard!

Green Mamba

They climb through the trees . . . hide in grass and among rocks . . .

Sidewinder

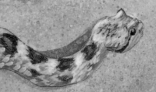

and glide across the sand.

Some even swim in oceans, lakes, and rivers!

Banded Sea Snake

**'s Live In...**

- Jungles
- Deserts
- Swamps
- Forests
- Grass, rocks, trees, and sand
- Oceans, lakes, rivers
- Underground

At the approach of the cold season, some snakes find a hole or den to sleep in until it becomes warm again.

129

WHAT DO SNAKES EAT?

They eat meat! That's why they are called **carnivores**—a big word that means meat-eaters.

Copperhead

Most snakes feed on small animals. But larger snakes can eat big animals!

Mexican Milk Snake

's Eat

- Insects and worms
- Frogs and lizards
- Mice, rats, and rabbits
- Birds
- Larger animals
- Other snakes

Some snakes
eat other snakes!

HOW DO SNAKES CATCH AND KILL THEIR FOOD?

Asp Viper

Snakes are sneaky! Sometimes they hide and wait for a meal to pass by. Other times they creep up on an animal—and attack with their sharp teeth! Some snakes use their big, hollow fangs to give victims a shot of deadly venom.

One kind of cobra can blind animals by spitting venom into their eyes.

Cobra

133

Some snakes use their big, strong bodies to **SQUEEZE** the life out of an animal. This is called **constriction**.

How 🐍's Get Food
- Sharp teeth
- Poison
- Constriction

Emerald Tree Boa

It's kind of like when your aunt comes to visit—and gives you a killer hug!

HOW DO SNAKES EAT AND DIGEST THEIR FOOD?

They always swallow a meal whole—sometimes while it is still alive!

It can take an hour to get a big animal into a snake's belly—and weeks to digest it! Snakes have very strong stomach juices that can dissolve even bones and teeth.

🐍's Eating and Digestion

- Swallow meals whole
- Use specially hinged, wide-opening jaws
- Have strong stomach juices

Ball Python

With its specially hinged jaws, a snake can swallow animals larger than its own head!

137

HOW DO SNAKES PROTECT THEMSELVES?

Any way they can! Snakes are great hunters—but sometimes they get hunted themselves. Large birds, crocodiles, and other animals love a tasty snake snack.

Sand Viper

Some hide by blending into their surroundings. This is called **camouflage**. Others are brightly colored to warn predators that they may be venomous!

Coral Snake

The rattlesnake will hiss loudly and rattle its tail to frighten enemies.

8

Rattlesnake

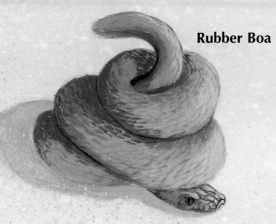

Rubber Boa

- Camouflage
- Bright warning colors
- Frightening sounds
- Curling up
- Playing dead
- Moving quickly

The rubber boa curls into a ball and hides its head if attacked.

Black Mamba

The black mamba moves as fast as 7 miles (11 km) per hour to escape predators.

Hognose Snake

And the hognose snake rolls over and plays dead!

13

HOW DO SNAKES GROW UP?

Most hatch from eggs. The eggs are tough and leathery, not brittle like bird eggs. Some snakes give birth to live babies!

Newborn baby snakes can take care of themselves right away.

And just as you outgrow your clothes, snakes get too big for their scaly skins. Several times a year they have to **shed**, or peel their skin off. It comes off in one piece—just like a sock!

141

BET YOU DIDN'T KNOW...

Asian Reticulated Python

The Asian reticulated python is the longest snake—some reach lengths of 30 feet (9 m)!

The thread snake is the shortest snake. It is less than 5 inches (13 cm) long!

Thread Snake

The heaviest snake, weighing up to 600 pounds (272 kg), is the anaconda!

Pound for pound, snakes have more muscle than any other animal.

Gaboon Viper

Gaboon vipers have the largest fangs—up to 2 inches (5 cm) long!

Indonesian Flying Snake

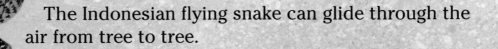

Sometimes snakes are born with two heads!

The Indonesian flying snake can glide through the air from tree to tree.

The African rock python can live up to 2 years without eating.

African Rock Python

We have 12 pairs of ribs; snakes have over 200 pairs!

Rough Green Snake

Long, skinny snakes have only one working lung— they don't have room for two!

DO SNAKES MAKE GOOD PETS?

It depends on you and your family. But a few of these animals—garter, king, and corn snakes, for example—are easy to keep. And, if treated properly, they can become one of the most interesting pets you'll ever own!

144

KNOW·IT·ALLS®

Spiders!

There are more than 35,000 different kinds of them. They can be found almost everywhere. They are one of the few animals in the world that use traps to catch prey. And they have been the stars of hundreds of scary movies.

What are they?

(Hint: turn the
page to find out . . .)

Answer:
SPIDERS!

What is a spider?

It is an **arachnid** (ah-RAK-nid)—a class of animal that includes scorpions and ticks.

Many people think that spiders are insects, but they are not.

148

Both insects and spiders have an **exoskeleton**, or hard shell, on the outside of their body. But unlike insects, spiders have only two separate body sections: the **cephalothorax** (sef-ah-lo-THOR-aks), which is the head and chest area, and the **abdomen**. (Insects have three body sections!)

Spiders are distant relatives of lobsters and crabs!

All spiders have eight legs—four on each side. (Insects only have six legs!)

wandering spider

Many spiders have sharp claws on their feet that help them climb!

Body Parts

- Exoskeleton
- Two sections: cephalothorax and abdomen
- Eight legs
- Up to eight eyes
- Fangs

wolf spider

And speaking of eight, spiders have up to eight eyes! They also have fangs that they use when they eat.

151

What do spiders eat?

Anything they are big enough to catch! That's why most spiders feed on insects and sometimes other spiders.

wolf spider

Big spiders have big appetites! Some are large enough to eat mice, frogs, lizards, and small birds!

's Eat

- Insects
- Other spiders
- Fish
- Mice
- Frogs and lizards
- Small birds

tarantula

But no matter the size, every spider uses its fangs to inject venom. The venom paralyzes or kills the victim. Then the spider sucks out its body juices. Spiders can't chew, so they only "eat" liquids.

153

Where do spiders live?

Everywhere! Spiders are found in all areas of the world—forests, deserts, the tropics, mountains, caves, even in the icy-cold Arctic! Some even live on the water's edge.

crab spider

tarantula

marbled orb weaver

fishing spider

Some spiders like to make their home in your home!

common house spider

's Live In
- Forests
- Deserts
- Tropical rainforests
- Mountains
- The Arctic
- Beaches
- Near lakes, streams, and ponds
- Caves
- In your home

How do spiders spin webs?

They use special body parts called **spinnerets** that are located in their abdomen! The spinnerets release long, sticky strands of silk thread. The spider weaves the silk strands together into a web!

banded garden spider

To make a web like this, a spider starts by making triangles that meet at the center. Then it weaves a circular pattern around that point.

Why do spiders spin webs?

For lots of reasons! Many spiders use their webs as homes—and to trap victims!

orb weaver

The orb weaver spins a big, sticky web to catch a meal. Insects fly into it and get stuck—and then they're spider food! (Too bad, fly!)

Australian funnel weaver

The funnel weaver spins a cone-shaped web and waits inside. When a victim comes into its funnel web—the spider strikes!

159

Some spiders, however, do not spin silk for homes or traps. The jumping spider spins a silk safety line when it makes a big jump! Although spiders do not have wings, they can sometimes sail through the air for great distances. As the wind carries them aloft, they simply let out longer and longer safety lines.

jumping spider

nursery web spider

Why 🕷's Spin Silk

- To build homes
- To catch other animals
- To make safety lines
- To travel great distances
- To protect eggs

wolf spider

The female nursery web spider wraps her eggs safely in a silk sack. Then she builds a "nursery" for the sack by folding over a leaf and tying it up with silk! It's just like a spider-baby bassinet!

161

Where do baby spiders come from?

Quickly turn back the page to find out! (Go ahead!) That's right—they hatch from eggs!

Baby spiders are called **spiderlings**. Some spiderlings ride on their mother's back until they are large and strong enough to be on their own.

black and yellow garden spider, with egg sack

female wolf spider

162

How 's Grow Up

- Hatch from eggs
- Some ride on mother's back
- Shed their skin as they grow

yellow crab spider
shedding outer shell

As they get bigger, spiderlings outgrow their exoskeletons—just like you outgrow an old pair of sneakers! And as they shed their hard shells, new ones form.

163

How do spiders protect themselves?

Usually by hiding! The trap-door spider stays inside a covered burrow most of the time. Others, like the crab spider, just blend into the background! That's called **camouflage.**

elegant crab spider

trapdoor spider

🕷 **Defenses**

- Camouflage
- Web lines
- Jumping
- Breaking off a leg
- "Itchy" hairs

A tarantula's hairs can make predators itch so they stay away!

jumping spider

Many spiders can drop quickly on web lines to avoid danger. Some jump to get away from enemies. And if all else fails, a spider may break off one of its legs to escape the grip of a hungry animal!

Bet you didn't know . . .

Jumping spiders can leap more than 50 times their own body length.

Ounce for ounce, the female black widow spider's venom is 15 times more deadly than that of a rattlesnake.

The water spider traps bubbles of air in a silken dome to breathe underwater!

Crab spiders can walk forward, backward, or even sideways!

The spitting spider spits sticky goo at victims to keep them from running away!

After mating, the female black widow often eats the male!

Spiders are cool! There's really no reason not to like them . . .

Spiders spin different kinds of silk—some sticky and nonsticky. (They walk on the nonsticky silk, and use the sticky silk to trap victims!)

unless
you're a fly!

KNOW·IT·ALLS

BUGS!

Written by
Christopher Nicholas

Illustrated by
Mike Maydak

They walk, crawl, swim, and fly all over the world. There are more of them than any other kind of animal on Earth! And they have been around for over 350 million years!

What are they?

(Hint: turn the
page to find out ...)

What makes an insect an insect?

For one thing, it has a special body. All insects have a hard shell on the outside called an **exoskeleton**. The shell protects the little insect just like metal armor protects a knight!

Ladybug

Earwig

172

Grasshopper

Ant

An insect's body also has three parts. It has a head, a middle section called a thorax, and an abdomen. These three parts are easy to see on one insect that everyone knows—the ant.

People have two legs. Dogs and cats have four legs—and insects have SIX! (Go ahead, count them!) But not all insect legs are the same. Some legs are good for jumping far. Others are perfect for climbing, grabbing, running, or swimming.

Grasshopper

Praying Mantis

Spiders have eight legs. They are NOT insects!

Dragonfly

Most insects have two or four wings. And just like legs, there are different kinds of wings. The dragonfly's big wings are perfect for flying fast and making quick turns in mid-air! But a beetle's wings are different—one pair is thick and leathery to protect the second pair of delicate flight wings.

Beetle

175

As you can see, bugs are a lot different from you and me. And speaking of "seeing," did you know that insects have two different types of eyes? An insect's **simple eyes**, called "ocelli," can only sense light. Their larger, **compound eyes** can see objects and animals and their movements.

Fly

A housefly's compound eyes have thousands of little parts called lenses. Each lens sees a piece of a bigger picture. What would an apple look like to a fly?

What is sticking out of that bug's head? They're feelers or "antennae." And all insects have two of them. They help insects touch, taste, and smell the world around them.

Where do insects live?

Everywhere! They fly through the air and walk on the ground. They dig in the dirt and hide under rocks. They climb through the trees and swim in water. Some insects even live in your home!

Damselfly

Common stone fly

Harlequin bug
with eggs

Waterstrider

Orange stone fly

Some insects, like the flea, make themselves at home on other animals!

Butterfly

Pallid wing grasshopper

Bee

Milkweed bug

179

Bees

People live together in groups called families. Some insects live together in groups, too. Ants, bees, and termites live in groups called **colonies.**

Ants

Where 🪲's Live

- In the air
- On the ground
- In dirt
- Under rocks
- In trees
- In and around water
- Some live together in colonies or hives

Termites

Each member of an insect group has a special job. Some find and gather food. Some build and dig. Others take care of the young.

Termites eat wood from trees—and from your house!

181

What do insects eat?

Some eat leaves and stems from plants and trees. **MUNCH!** Others suck nectar and juice from flowers and fruit. **SLURP!** And some insects like to eat other insects! **CRUNCH!**

Butterfly

Ladybug

Aphids

Ladybug larvae

Some insects drink blood from other animals—like you and me! **OUCH!** Other insects, like the cockroach and the fly, eat garbage, animal waste, and other dead things. **YUCK!** But they recycle garbage to keep the earth clean!

Mosquito

Fly

Cockroach

The little silverfish likes to eat paper. Keep him away from this book!

What 's Eat
- Plants
- Other insects
- Blood
- Wood and paper
- Garbage, animal waste, and other dead things

183

How do insects "talk" to each other?

Ants communicate through smells. They use odors to warn their nest mates of danger and to lead them to food.

Ants

Other insects send messages with movement! When a bee finds food, it will do a little dance in the nest to tell the other bees "it's time to eat!"

Bees

Many insects communicate with sounds. Male field crickets chirp by rubbing their wings together to attract a female cricket. Fireflies find each other with flashes of light!

Fireflies

How 's "TALK"
- Smells and scents
- Motion
- Sound
- Light

Cricket

Wasp

How do insects protect themselves?

Wasps use poison stings to fight off predators. Other insects wear special armor.

Goldsmith beetle

Stink bug

Giant walking stick

Scarlet and green leafhoppers

A few insects, like the stink bug, spray stinky liquids at their enemies. They are the skunks of the insect world!

Many insects have colors that blend with the places they live. This is called **camouflage**. Can you find the insects that color helps hide on this page?

187

How does an insect grow up?

All insects hatch from eggs. As they grow, they get bigger and begin to look more like their parents. (Just like you!)

Egg

Larva (Caterpillar)

The change that insects go through from egg to adult is called **metamorphosis**. That's a big word that means "changes shape."

188

There are different kinds of metamorphosis. Some insects change by just growing bigger. Others grow wings. But there are some insects, such as butterflies, that change so much that the adult looks nothing like the youth.

Pupa (Chrysalis)

Adult

How 's Grow Up

- All hatch from eggs
- All go through metamorphosis

Bet you didn't know. . .

Flies can taste with their feet!

When in flight, a mosquito beats its wings 300 times in a single second!

The waterstrider can actually walk on water!

A flea can jump over 200 times its own length!

One ladybug can lay up to 1500 eggs in her lifetime!

Cockroaches are so smart that they have learned to run mazes in laboratories!

The giant water bug has been known to eat tadpoles and small fish!

A dragonfly can fly as fast as 30 miles (48 km) per hour!

Some bee hives have up to 50,000 bees!

Insects are amazing! But do you know what my favorite thing about them is? (Hint: turn the page to find out . . .)

A cricket can hear with its legs!

They're small!

192

KNOW-IT-ALLS

Butterflies!

In the spring, crawling caterpillars appear, munching on plants. Soon butterflies fill the air, flitting from flower to flower. Have you ever wondered where all those hungry caterpillars and beautiful butterflies come from?

Turn the page
to find out!

195

Life Cycle of a Butterfly

One of the most amazing transformations in nature happens as a butterfly grows. It completely changes the way it looks! This change is called **metamorphosis** (met-uh-MOR-foh-sis). This cycle has four steps.

Gulf Fritillary egg

196

Chalcedon
Checkerspot
eggs

European Cabbage
White eggs

1. Eggs

A butterfly begins its life as an egg. Most female
butterflies lay their eggs on the kinds of plants their
caterpillars will want to eat. Some butterfly eggs hatch
in a few days. Others hatch in a few months.

2. The Caterpillar

When the butterfly **larva** (LAR-vah), better known as a caterpillar, hatches from the egg, it has an ENORMOUS appetite. It usually begins by eating its own eggshell! Then, with its oversized jaws, called **mandibles**, it begins to eat plants.

Gulf Fritillary
hatching from egg

mandibles

198

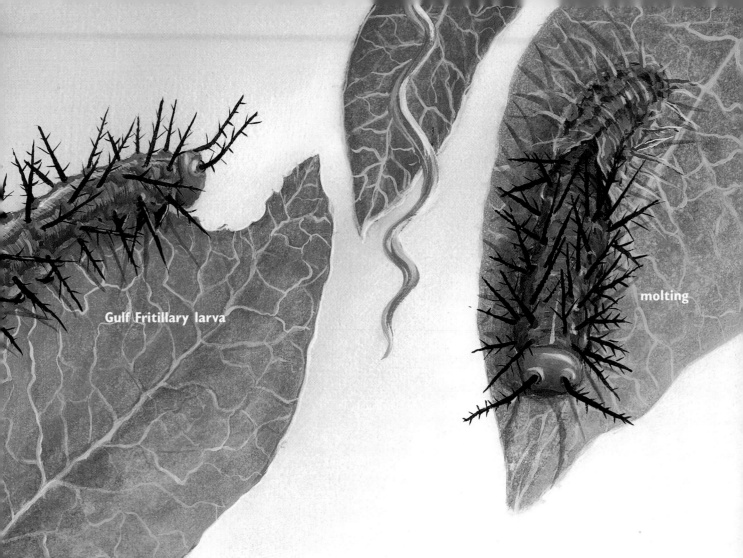

Gulf Fritillary larva

molting

The caterpillar eats . . . and eats . . . and *EATS*! It finally gets too big for its own skin! When this happens, the old skin splits open and the caterpillar crawls out of it wearing a new skin. This is called **molting**.

199

3. The Pupa

The caterpillar spins silk and then attaches itself to a twig.

The caterpillar molts. It emerges as a prepupa.

When a caterpillar reaches full size, it molts to reveal a soft new body called a prepupa. Its soft, tender body slowly hardens to form a **chrysalis** (KRIS-uh-lis).

Its soft body becomes a chrysalis.

The butterfly is in its third stage of metamorphosis, the pupa.

Inside this hard shell, the insect, now called a **pupa**, changes into an adult butterfly. This transformation can take a few days for some kinds of butterflies or up to a year for others.

201

4. The Adult

When the adult butterfly is fully formed, the chrysalis cracks open. The butterfly frees itself from the hard shell.

Metamorphosis

- Hatches from an egg
- Molts as the caterpillar grows
- Forms a chrysalis in the pupa stage
- Emerges from chrysalis as an adult

Monarch

At first, its wings are soft and crumpled. The butterfly pumps blood into its wings so that they will spread and harden. In an hour or two, it is ready to fly!

203

Butterfly Body Parts

Like all insects, butterflies have six legs and three main body parts: a **head**, a **thorax**, and an **abdomen**.

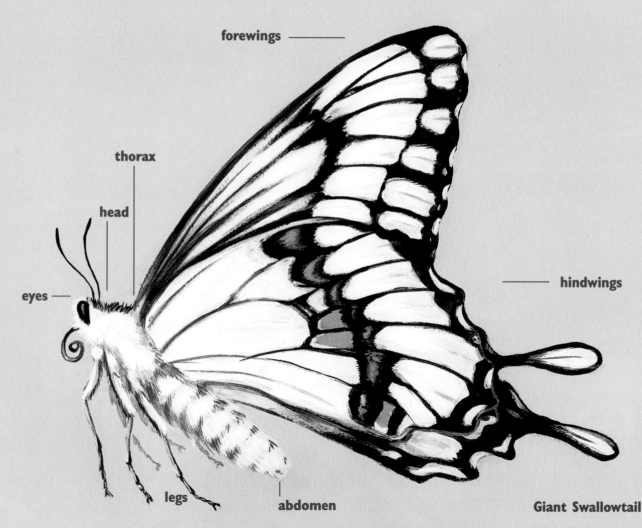

forewings

thorax

head

eyes

hindwings

legs

abdomen

Giant Swallowtail

antennae

proboscis

Eastern Tiger Swallowtail

Butterflies have special sensors, called **antennae** (an-TEN-e), on their heads. They drink with a long tongue called a **proboscis** (pro-BOSS-sis) and use wings to fly.

205

Butterfly Life

All butterflies eat with their proboscis. Some sip flower nectar, tree sap, or the salts and minerals from damp soil and puddles. Others may drink the liquid from decaying animals, fruit, and animal droppings.

Clearwing

Gray Hairstreak

Thousands of tiny scales on each wing give a butterfly its colors. Butterflies are a type of insect called **Lepidoptera** (lep-eh-DOP-terah), which means "scaly wings"!

Butterflies find food and locate a mate with their eyes, "smell" and sense vibrations with their antennae, and taste with their front feet!

Postman Butterfly

Peacock Butterflies

During the winter some butterflies hibernate in caves, under leaves, inside houses, and in other safe places.

A Long Journey

Several different kinds of butterflies **migrate** (MY-grate). That means they travel long distances from one place to another each year. The Monarch is one of the most famous migrating butterflies in North America.

Monarch

Fact

- Monarchs migrate thousands of miles.

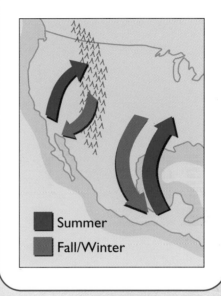

Summer

Fall/Winter

In the fall when the weather gets cold, swarms of Monarch butterflies migrate from as far north as Canada to sunny California and Mexico. In the spring, they lay their eggs which hatch. The new butterflies fly back north—the round-trip is almost 4,000 miles (6,436 km) long. Those Monarchs lay more eggs that hatch and begin the journey south again!

209

Masters of Disguise

Butterflies need to protect themselves from birds, lizards, monkeys, spiders, and other predators. Some butterflies have colors and patterns on their wings that help them stay hidden.

They can appear to be part of a rock, a leaf, a tree, a flower, or something else in their environment. This is called **camouflage** (KA-ma-flahj).

Can you find the three butterflies hidden on this page?

Other Defenses

Butterflies can defend themselves in many other ways.

Viceroy, a mimic

Monarch

Some butterflies, such as the Monarch, taste bad. Other butterflies, called **mimics**, just happen to look like them. Predators leave them both alone rather than eat the wrong one!

female

male

In some butterfly families, the males are more colorful than the females. Predators see and eat more of the males, so more females survive to lay eggs!

Defenses

- Camouflage
- Bad taste and smell
- Mimicry
- Wing spots
- Flashy colors

Owl Butterfly

Wing spots that look like eyes or flashy coloring can startle predators and give the butterfly a chance to escape.

**Old World
Swallowtail
caterpillar**

Some caterpillars use unpleasant odors to drive predators away.

213

Bet you didn't know...

Overall, the Queen Alexandria Birdwing is the biggest butterfly in the world. It's twice as big as this picture!

The Western Pygmy Blue is one of the smallest butterflies. Its wings are only 3/8 inch (1 cm) across. This picture is twice as big as a real Western Pygmy Blue!

Some caterpillars have eyespots and other markings that make them look like a little snake.

Spicebush Swallowtail

The Question Mark is a curious little butterfly that has markings on its wings that look like question marks.

Some swallowtail caterpillars make tents out of leaves for shelter.

215

Butterflies Everywhere!

Purplish Copper

Monarch

Common Swallowtail

Regal Fritillary

Cabbage White

Common Sulfer

There are over 10,000 named species of butterflies in the world—and many more left to be discovered! You would have to find 10 different species a day for three years to come close to seeing them all. Better start looking now!

216

KNOW-IT-ALLS

HORSES!

They have thundered wild across the American Southwest. They've been the loyal companions of cavalry, cowboys, and kings alike. They've worked on farms and have even been used to help deliver fresh milk door to door!

what are they?

(Hint: Turn the page to find out...)

Answer: HORSES!

The horse belongs to the species Equus caballus. It is a hardy, four-legged mammal. Each leg has one toe that is protected by a hard covering, called a **hoof**, which is a lot like a really thick toenail.

First **domesticated**, or tamed, by people almost 6,000 years ago, these strong animals have been bred to help us everywhere from the farm to the battlefield. Since then, horses have also been raised for sport and show.

American Quarter Horse

zebra   Poitou donkey   mule

Horses, zebras, and donkeys are all related. They belong to the same animal family that scientists call Equidae. A mule is a crossbreed of a horse and a donkey.

How many types of horses are there?

While there are many different kinds, or **breeds**, of horses, they can be divided into three main groups: heavy horses, light horses, and ponies.

Large, muscular horses are called **heavy breeds**. They are usually the biggest and tallest horses. Originally bred in northern Europe during the Middle Ages, they were used for carrying heavy loads and for pulling ploughs to till fields.

The heavy horses were also used for battle. Sometimes they wore armor just like the medieval knights who rode them!

Light horses are skinnier looking than the heavy breeds. They are bred for speed, agility, and stamina. Though most light horses are used for work such as pulling carriages and ranching, some are used in races and show competitions.

Ponies are often thought to be baby horses, but they are actually breeds of horses that are much shorter – even when fully grown.

229

A horse's eyes sit high on its long head. They are positioned to give the horse a wide field of vision, which is perfect for seeing other animals sneaking up from the sides or behind to hunt it for food. But the eyes also face forward so the horse can see whatever might be in front of it.

The ears of a horse, also high on its head, can be controlled independently to allow the horse to figure out where sounds are coming from.

Horses use their tails to swat away pesky insects.

Like many other animals, horses use their sense of smell to help them find food and water — and to recognize family, friends, and enemies.

How big are horses?

A horse is measured in **hands** from the ground to the top of its shoulders, called the **withers**. A hand is about 4 inches (10.2 cm) long, which is about the width of an adult's hand.

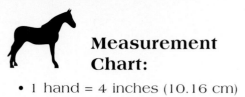

Measurement Chart:

- 1 hand = 4 inches (10.16 cm)
- 14.2 hands (14 hands plus 2 inches) = 58 inches (147.3 cm)
- 16 hands = 64 inches (162.6 cm)

Ponies are generally less than 14.2 hands high.

American Saddlebred (average height: 15 to 16 hands)

Shetland pony (average height: 9.3 hands)

Most light horses are
14.2 to 16 hands high.

Heavy breeds usually stand
more than 16 hands high.

Shire
(average height:
17 hands)

*Averaging
17 hands high, the Shire is the
largest horse. One Shire, named King,
holds the record for being the tallest
horse at 19.2 hands!*

How do horses live?

Horses are social animals. In the wild, they live with their families in larger groups called **herds**. Most herds are made up of male and female horses, but some are all male. A dominant male horse, called a **stallion**, usually leads the herd. The stallion acts as the protector.

There are very few types of undomesticated horses left in the world. Only the Przewalski's horse of Mongolia and untamed horses, called **feral** horses, still roam wild and free.

what do horses eat?

Horses are **herbivores**, which means they do not eat meat. They mostly graze on grass. Although grass is not very nutritious for people, it has everything horses need to stay strong and healthy.

A horse's mouth and front teeth are especially well formed for eating grass right from the ground. Its long jaws are lined with teeth that grind the grass to a fine pulp, making it easy to swallow and digest.

Food

- Grass
- Hay and grains
  (on farms)
- Other plants

How do baby horses grow?

Fast! A female horse, called a **mare**, usually gives birth to one baby at a time. The newborn horse, called a **foal**, can usually stand up within an hour of being born. Its legs may be unsteady at first, but soon it will be able to keep up with its mother at nearly full speed.

*A horse less than four years old is called a **colt**. Sometimes a female horse in this age range is called a **filly**.*

Like all mammals, the baby drinks milk from its mother. To get extra nutrition, it may nurse for up to a year, although it starts eating grass within a few weeks of being born.

Do horses really wear shoes?

Believe it or not, horses need shoes! Their hooves can get worn down and damaged during the work they do.

A blacksmith trims each hoof just like trimming a toenail. Then the blacksmith attaches an iron horseshoe with nails. The nails don't hurt the horse, and the shoe protects the hoof and keeps it healthy.

Horseshoes have been considered a sign of good luck for hundreds of years. One legend has it that Saint Dunstan the blacksmith gave the horseshoe special power against evil.

A blacksmith is someone who makes things out of metal by hand.

How do horses communicate?

Horses spend much of their time grooming each other to show affection, form friendships, and help each other clean up. But a horse may also nip at another horse to try to show that it is in charge.

Who's the boss?
Two domestic palominos
fight each other to
decide.

243

Bet you didn't know...

All horses can sleep standing up. This allows them to quickly run away from predators because they don't have to get up off the ground and to their feet. But horses also rest and sleep lying down when they feel safe and comfortable.

The horse is the only one-toed, one-hoofed creature on earth. All other hoofed animals, such as cows, have two or more toes and split hooves.

You may have seen pictures of Pegasus, a horse that had wings and could fly. But Pegasus was not real. No horse could ever fly.

Have you ever seen a zebroid? A zebroid is a crossbreed of a horse and a zebra.

Horses were once such an important part of life that the first trains were called iron horses and the first automobiles were called horseless carriages. Even today, the word "horsepower" is used to describe how much work the machine can do!

Engine-powered machines have replaced the horse in a number of ways, but horses have been our companion and helper for thousands of years . . .

239

... so I wouldn't say happy trails to the horse anytime soon, because grass will always be cheaper than gas!

KITTENS

They were worshipped as gods in ancient Egypt. Mighty lions and ferocious tigers are their cousins. And they like to play with balls of yarn.

What are they?

(Hint: Turn the page to find out...)

243

What is a kitten?

A kitten is a very young cat, just as a child is a very young person. Kittens are *mammals* like you and me. When they are babies, they feed on their mother's milk.

244

Cheetah

Tiger

Ocelot

Lion

African Wild Cat

Domestic Cat

As members of the cat family, kittens are related to lions, tigers, leopards, cheetahs, and other big cats that live in the wild. But most kittens are *domesticated*. That means, unlike their wild cousins, they live with and depend on people to take care of them.

All kittens are covered with thick hair, called **fur**, which protects them by keeping them warm and dry. Their ears allow them to hear high-pitched sounds that humans can't hear, like a mouse squeaking. And they have four legs and four fuzzy feet, called *paws*.

But watch out! Kittens also have sharp claws to help them climb, hunt, and fight.

A tail helps a kitten keep its balance when climbing and jumping – kind of the way an umbrella helps a tightrope walker stay balanced on the high wire.

Body Parts

- Four legs and paws
- Claws
- Whiskers
- Four canines (long, pointy teeth)

Kittens are specially equipped for the dark. Big, shiny eyes help them see better, and long whiskers act as "feelers" to help them find their way.

How many types of kittens are there?

Red Persian Longhair

There are more than 250 different kinds, or *breeds*, of kittens in the world. Each breed has a very distinctive size, shape, fur length, and color. But all the breeds fall under two types.

Long-Haired Kittens

Black Turkish Angora

Some kittens barely have hair at all!

Short-Haired Kittens

Sphynx

British Blue Shorthair

Siamese

How are kittens born?

How a 🐈 is Born
- One at a time
- Average litter: 2-6

When a mother cat is ready to have her kittens, she finds a safe, quiet place, such as under a bed or inside a closet. The mother cat can give birth to as many as seven or eight kittens – two to six is more typical. Together, the kittens are called a *litter*.

Mother cats lick their kittens to bathe them and teach them how to clean their own fur when they get older.

Licking also helps a kitten's skin glands produce more body oil to waterproof its coat. That's why they're always so shiny!

To bathe themselves, cats and older kittens lick their paws and use them to wash areas like their heads and faces where their tongues can't reach.

Food

- Mother's milk
- Packaged kitten food
- Meat from small animals

What do kittens eat?

When they are first born, kittens mostly drink milk from their mothers. By the time they're eight weeks old, they are big enough to eat solid food – either kitten food from their pet owners or small animals caught by their mother.

How do kittens grow?

Little by little – just like you do!

Newborn kittens weigh three or four ounces (85 or 113.4 grams), and they are so tiny that you can hold one in the palm of your hand. Born with their eyes and ears closed, they have a good sense of smell.

In a week, the kittens grow twice their original size! Then, nine to 20 days later, their eyes and ears begin to open. Because the kittens cannot stand or walk, the mother cat carries them around in her mouth.

When do kittens become cats?

After four weeks, the kittens stand and slowly begin to walk. Still wobbly, they wander off and explore. But mom always keeps a close cat eye on them!

By eight to 12 weeks, the kittens' bodies are longer and stronger. They can run, play, and get into all kinds of kitty mischief.

Development

4 Weeks:
• Stand
• Start walking

8-12 Weeks:
• Run
• Play

6 Months:
• Nearly full-grown
• Independent

Finally, after six months, the kittens are nearly full-grown. They can do everything that adult cats can do! And they are ready to take care of themselves and lead their own cat lives.

257

Why do kittens play so much?

Because it comes naturally to them.

Cats and kittens that live in the wild hunt mice and other small animals for food. So domestic kittens that chase balls, poke in and out of boxes, and climb on curtains are actually practicing mouse hunting!

Behavior

- Naturally curious
- Playful (practice for hunting and fighting)

258

And when kittens wrestle with each other, they are learning how to protect themselves from other animals.

How do kittens communicate?

In many different ways. You just have to listen – and look!

Kittens meow to say "hello," or to ask for something. And they purr when they are happy. When they're scared or angry, kittens hiss, puff out their fur, and arch their backs to make themselves look bigger – and scarier.

A kitten's ears and tail can also show you what it's thinking.

Ears

Up and forward = happy
Back = angry
Flat = afraid

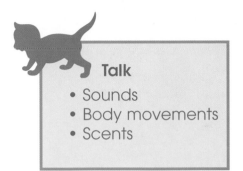

Talk
- Sounds
- Body movements
- Scents

Tail

Straight and high = happy
Waving = excited or nervous
Down = sad or scared

Kittens also use smells to communicate. They rub against people and things to leave their scent and mark their territory. It says to other animals, "This is mine. Stay away!"

Bet you didn't know...

Kittens can see in light six times dimmer than people.

Where'd they go? Kittens can pull in, or *retract*, their front claws.

Kittens almost always land on their feet! They have a special organ in their middle ear that helps them tell which side is up.

A kitten's whiskers grow to be a little longer than the width of its body.

Kittens are great at climbing up, but they have a very hard time climbing down.

Kittens are tons of furry fun! But always remember to play nice . . .

. . . because you wouldn't want to make their big cousins angry!

KNOW-IT ALLS

WILD CATS!

Have you ever seen a cat go after a toy mouse, or try to catch a bird?

With their good eyesight and hearing—and sharp teeth and claws—house cats are a lot like their relatives, the big cats.

And big cats often look like giant house cats when
they take a nap under a tree, or roll in the grass!

LION

The lion is often called the king of the beasts. It has a beautiful mane of golden hair, huge teeth, and . . . a very loud roar!

The lion grows up to 10 feet (3 meters) long. It weighs as much as 500 pounds (229 kg). Its queen, the lioness, weighs 300 pounds (137 kg). That's a lot more than most grown men weigh!

Lions are the only cats that live in family groups, called **prides**. It is the male lion's job to keep the pride safe.

FACT

Homeland: Africa; Gir Forest, NW India

Remember: It is the only cat that lives in groups!

269

Lions hunt as a group. That way, they're able to kill animals larger than themselves—such as wildebeests, or even young elephants or giraffes.

They can charge their prey at 40-50 miles (64.5 to 81 km) per hour. That's as fast as a car moving on a highway! Even though females do most of the hunting, the males get to eat first.

Lionesses give birth to as many as five or six babies, called **cubs**. The cubs stay close to their mother for up to two years.

Lion cubs spend lots of time chasing and pouncing on each other. This is how they learn to defend themselves and hunt. Once they're grown, males leave their sisters and mother behind to form their own pride.

273

TIGER

What's larger, heavier, and more ferocious than a lion? A tiger—it is the biggest cat of all!

The male Siberian tiger weighs over 600 pounds (275 kg). It can grow to be 14 feet long (4 meters), nose to tail. That is twice as long as your living-room sofa!

Tigers live on the continent of Asia. They live in steamy hot places. And they live in very cold places, where their coats are extra thick to keep them warm.

FACT

Homeland: Asia

Remember: It is the largest cat!

Tigers usually live by themselves. Their stripes help hide them in long grasses and dark forests. Each tiger has its own special stripe pattern.

Tigers eat water buffalo, cattle, and antelope. But if they're not lucky enough to catch a big animal, they'll settle for a frog! Tigers are good swimmers. They often wait for their prey near a waterhole.

LEOPARD

The leopard is the smallest of the big cats. It weighs about 100 pounds (46 kg). If you ever go to leopard country, look up in the trees! You might see a leopard in one. Leopards are very good climbers.

FACT

Homeland: Southern Asia, Africa

Remember: It is the smallest big cat!

This mother leopard is carrying her cub by the loose skin of its neck. Don't worry—it doesn't hurt the cub at all!

The **"black panther"** is actually a **leopard**. It is born with black spots on a black background.

Unlike the other big cats, leopards don't usually roar—the sound they make is more of a raspy call.

SNOW LEOPARD

The snow leopard has a woolly whitish-gray coat that blends in with the snow. Its long tail comes in handy as a thick scarf! The snow leopard has always been hunted for its fur. It is very endangered today.

Snow leopards can grow to be seven feet (2 meters) long, from head to fluffy tail. They're excellent jumpers. They hunt goats, ground squirrels, antelopes, and even cattle!

FACT

Homeland: Central Asia

Remember: It loves the cold!

CLOUDED LEOPARD

The clouded leopard is not a true big cat, because it doesn't roar. It purrs!

But like big cats, it does have very long teeth. And like its distant relative the true leopard, it also climbs trees.

FACT

Homeland: Southeast Asia

Remember: It purrs!

CHEETAH

The cheetah is the "sports car" of cats. When a cheetah hunts, it moves in for the kill in a burst of speed. In only two seconds, it goes from 0 to 45 miles (0 to 72.5 km) per hour. In a few seconds, it speeds up to 70 miles (113 km) per hour! But it can only run that fast for a short time.

JAGUAR

The jaguar is a strong cat with short, sturdy legs. Males may grow as large as eight feet (2.5 meters) long. The jaguar is a good leaper and pouncer—especially when it's hungry! It likes to hunt sloths and tapirs. Since it's a good swimmer, it catches turtles and fish, too.

Jaguars don't roar very much. They tend to grunt, cough, and growl instead!

FACT

Homeland: South America

Remember: It is the largest South American cat!

Which big cat is your favorite?

The cheetah has a slim, doglike body. Its flexible spine works like a spring to shoot the cheetah forward. Powerful back legs, large lungs, and extra-long claws help make the cheetah the fastest land animal in the world.

FACT

Homeland: Africa

Remember: It is the fastest land animal in the world!